The Little book of

M   ds

Written by Sally Featherstone
Illustrations by Marion Lindsay

LITTLE BOOKS WITH BIG IDEAS

Published 2009 by A&C Black Publishers Limited
36 Soho Square, London W1D 3QY
www.acblack.com

ISBN 9781408114308

Printed in Great Britain by Latimer Trend & Company Limited.

This book is produced using paper that is made from wood grown in
managed, sustainable forests. It is natural, renewable and recyclable.

The logging and manufacturing processes conform to the environmental
regulations of the country of origin.

**To see our full range of titles
visit www.acblack.com**

Contents

Introduction

What are books and cards for?

Principles

Making books and cards, and sharing them with others, are activities that have the following benefits:

▶ The activity promotes independence, individuality and personalisation. Every letter and card is different, and can promote a feeling of self-worth and self-esteem.

▶ Making books, writing letters and sending messages are all models of communication in action and for real purposes, moving away from empty writing exercises, and giving children a genuine means of communicating for themselves and to others.

▶ Free access to letter and book-making resources and equipment, and systematic teaching of the associated skills will embed communication into your setting, so it becomes a self-initiated activity, needing little or no support from an adult.

▶ Card, letter and book making raises the profile of other languages, communities and celebrations, giving children with English as an additional language opportunities to share their languages, cultures and customs.

The activities in this book will also give children a chance to:

▶ learn about new techniques and how to use them

▶ acquire new skills through direct teaching, coaching and support

▶ watch adults as they model skills and activities

▶ get things out and put them away safely and tidily

▶ explore and talk about new resources, materials and fabrics

▶ play with new resources, skills and equipment

▶ talk about other people, make things for them, and plan for and make their own creations

▶ look at examples of creativity in books, pictures and on the Internet

▶ talk about what things are for and how to do things

▶ recognise their own and others' achievements in creating and sharing the books and cards they make

▶ include books and card making in their child-chosen activities

▶ contribute to the setting and their families by making objects and small gifts that support strong relationships and recognise the special relationship between children, their families and others in the setting.

Making room for messages and books

Every Early Years setting should provide free access to mark making and construction activities, including making books and cards.

Here are some ideas for making the areas of your room inviting and enriching for children who wish to make their own cards and books.

Your book corner

Make this area inviting for reading, and for making books, by providing plenty of resources.

Always display the books children make. Create space for them in the book corner, read them at story times and let the children take them home to show to their families.

Look at your book stock regularly and remove books that are old or worn, and particularly those that are damaged. You can offer the pages or pictures from these to the children for recycling into new books of their own, but remember to be clear about which books are available for cutting up!

Make a space or have a special board for information about celebrations – this could include bought and home-made cards to inspire new ideas, photos, books and other objects related to the current focus of celebration.

Mark making, construction or writing area

A wide range of interesting materials will stimulate curiosity in making books, cards, labels and other artefacts. Have plenty of examples of cards and other celebratory objects to stimulate interest, and refresh the resources regularly to maintain appeal.

You could have:

- ▶ a celebrations photo book, with photos of birthdays, new babies, Mother's Day, Easter, Diwali etc.
- ▶ a slip-folder with examples of different sorts of greeting card. Get samples from bargain shops and ask friends, colleagues and families to donate those they receive
- ▶ a postcard collection
- ▶ some little ready-made books – just a few blank sheets stapled together – ready for stories and pictures
- ▶ a list or calendar of everyone's birthday, so it's easy to remember whose birthday is coming up
- ▶ a range of different sizes and types of envelope
- ▶ headed or decorated notepaper to inspire letter writing
- ▶ lists of the children's names to make messages easier
- ▶ copies of photos of individual children.

Outside

Make sure there are opportunities for writing out of doors by providing resources in baskets, trolleys or boxes.

Encourage the children to make banners and flags for celebrations, writing big messages, letters and shapes on old sheets, pillowcases or fabric oddments.

Blackboards and big sheets of card can be fixed outside for big messages and reminders of celebrations and birthdays. Use easels and flip charts for big writing, lists, directions, adverts and posters.

Once you have taught the children how to make books, cards and messages, they will need plenty of practice in free play, so resources for these activities should be both plentiful and varied. We have included a list of some of the resources you may wish to collect for free play as well as more directed work.

Implements and tools for making books and cards

It's important to have effective tools and equipment for children to use in creative work. Cutting or stapling with blunt or inappropriate tools will lead to frustration for you and for them. Children's tools must be fit for purpose, and you may decide to use small versions of adult tools to supplement those made specifically for children. You will also need some adult tools, so you can prepare and model the skills you are expecting the children to acquire.

A tool box or basket should include the following:

Essential	Specialist
▶ sharp, round-ended children's scissors ▶ adult scissors (scissors for paper and fabric should be kept separate – paper and card blunt scissors very quickly) ▶ staplers – electric staplers are cheap and easy for children to use ▶ hole punch ▶ blunt needles	▶ left-handed and 'teaching' scissors ▶ long-arm stapler

Make sure you check all your tools regularly to ensure they are still sharp and working well. Watch the children as they work, and if they are having difficulty or getting frustrated, make sure they have the tools they need and know how to use them. Remove the build-up of glue and paint by washing scissors and brushes.

What you do

1. Introduce the concept and explore the contents of the bag. Which is the happy mask? How do we know? What emotions do the other masks show? Look at the books.

2. Explain that you can tell the Worry Bear anything that makes you happy or sad, excited or frightened. Invite the children to think of a name for the bear.

3. Talk to the children about how they feel. What do they like doing at nursery/school. What makes them happy and what makes them sad? How do we look when we are happy/sad?

4. Make happy/sad/cross/tired faces at each other. Look in the mirror at all the different faces you can make.

Further activities and curriculum links:

▶ Keep a daily chart of how we feel. The children fill this by drawing smiley/sad faces or putting stickers by their name. This can be a valuable activity for children with Special Educational needs or who may be experiencing difficulties at home or at school. (PSED)

▶ Keep the emotions sack readily available. The children can then access the bag independently and share with each other how they are feeling. (PSED)

And another idea...

▶ Find an alliterative name for your worry bear – William or Wilma Worry bear or a Caring bear – Cara or Kieran.

▶ Make alliterative names for the children: Jumping Jack, Laughing Lisa. Children love this game!

Some suggested papers and card types for your store cupboard:

► plain card in white and a range of colours	► envelopes
► recycled card from cereal packets or other packaging	► tissue and crêpe papers
	► kitchen foil
► foil-covered card	► stamps (used ones from letters work well)
► paper of all colours and thicknesses	► computer labels
► felt	► wrapping papers of all sorts (recycle your Christmas and birthday paper)
► thin foam	
► postcards	► calendars
► diaries	► wallpaper
► notebooks	► tissue paper
► sketchbooks	► *Post-it* notes in all sorts and sizes
► scrapbooks	

The activity pages

This book is in two sections:

Section 1 – Cards, notes, messages and letters

Section 2 – Making simple books.

Each activity page follows the same format, starting with **a book to get you started**, to read with the children as you explore a new technique or skill. This is followed by step-by-step instructions for:

► What you need

► What you do

► And another idea... (extensions and further activities)

► Some additional books and resources relevant to the activity

► Two or three major links with the EYFS goals, so you can be sure that the children are working towards relevant skills and knowledge.

Children will often want to return to an activity they have done with you by including it in their child-initiated play. If you teach them how to use and take care of the tools and equipment you will be able to leave an activity you have done with a small group for further free exploration with minimum adult supervision. Some of the best experiences follow skilled adult support, when children revisit the activities in their own play.

Adults should work alongside children, making their own versions of books and cards, talking about the processes and difficulties and sharing the enjoyment of telling stories, and writing and making simple books. This will reinforce the value of the activities, and will be particularly important for children who have English as an Additional Language or who come from homes where writing and reading are less obvious adult activities.

The following features of learning are all valuable in gaining and practising the skills needed for making books and cards.

▶ **Exploring and talking about new, recycled and familiar resources**.

▶ **Experiencing the pleasures of writing, sending and receiving letters, and writing books and diaries**.

▶ **Introducing new tools** and techniques and teaching children how to use them.

▶ **Looking at examples of creativity in diaries, books, letters and pictures**.

▶ **Free play** with new resources and equipment.

▶ **Talking about how to do things**, about concentrating, doing difficult things and about sometimes needing help.

▶ **Adult modelling of skills and activities** so children can see how they are done, but without implying that children will be able to perfect the skill immediately, or that there is only one right way of doing things.

▶ **Getting things out and putting them away** safely and tidily.

▶ **Acquiring new skills** with adult support for the process.

▶ **Having their achievements recognised** in words and expressions, and by having their creations displayed, shared and used by others.

▶ **Becoming independent and creative thinkers,** using their own ideas and taking these in new directions.

▶ **Selecting their own materials and resources and using them in self-chosen activities**.

▶ **Giving children opportunities to contribute to the setting and their families** by making letters, cards and books to share with others.

Links with the EYFS

The following goals are relevant to the activities in this book. They naturally include **Communication, Language and Literacy**, **Creative Development** and **Knowledge and Understanding of the World**, but we must also recognise the contribution that language activities make to **Personal, Social and Emotional Development**.

CLL: Communication, Language and Literacy
Language for communication and thinking

▶ Initiates communication with others, displaying greater confidence in more informal contexts.

▶ Talks activities through, reflecting on and modifying actions.

▶ Interacts with others in a variety of contexts, negotiating plans and activities, and taking turns in conversation.

▶ Uses talk to organise, sequence and clarify thinking, ideas, feelings and events, exploring the meanings and sounds of new words.

▶ Speaks clearly with confidence and control, showing awareness of the listener.

▶ Talks and listens confidently and with control, consistently showing awareness of the listener by including relevant detail.

▶ Uses language to work out and clarify ideas, showing control of a range of appropriate vocabulary.

Linking Sounds and Letters

▶ Joins in with rhyming and rhythmic activities.

▶ Shows an awareness of rhyme and alliteration.

▶ Links some sounds to letters.

▶ Links sounds to letters, naming and sounding letters of the alphabet.

▶ Hears and says sounds in words.

▶ Blends sounds in words.

▶ Uses phonic knowledge to read simple regular words.

▶ Attempts to read more complex words, using phonic knowledge.

▶ Uses knowledge of letters, sounds and words when reading and writing independently.

Reading

▶ Is developing an interest in books.

▶ Knows that print conveys meaning.

▶ Recognises a few familiar words.

▶ Knows that, in English, print is read from left to right and top to bottom.

▶ Shows an understanding of the elements of stories, such as main character, sequence of events and openings.

▶ Reads a range of familiar and common words and simple sentences independently.

▶ Retells narratives in the correct sequence, drawing on language patterns of stories.

▶ Shows an understanding of how information can be found in non-fiction texts to answer questions about where, who, why and how.

Writing

▶ Experiments with mark making, sometimes ascribing meaning to the marks.

▶ Uses some clearly identifiable letters to communicate meaning.

▶ Represents some sounds correctly in writing.

▶ Writes own name and other words from memory.

▶ Holds a pencil and uses it effectively to form recognisable letters, most of which are correctly formed.

▶ Attempts writing for a variety of purposes, using features of different forms.

▶ Uses phonic knowledge to write simple regular words and makes phonetically plausible attempts at more complex words.

▶ Begins to form captions and simple sentences, sometimes using punctuation.

▶ Communicates meaning through phrases and simple sentences with some consistency in punctuating them.

PSED: Personal, Social and Emotional Development

▶ Builds relationships through gesture and talk.

▶ Communicates freely about home and community.

▶ Responds to significant experiences, showing a range of feelings when appropriate.

▶ Has a developing awareness of own needs, views and feelings, and is sensitive to the needs, views and feelings of others.

▶ Understands that there need to be agreed values and codes of behaviour for groups of people, including adults and children, to work together harmoniously.

▶ Has a developing respect for own culture and beliefs, and those of other people.

▶ Understands that people have different needs, views, cultures and beliefs that need to be treated with respect.

▶ Understand that they can expect others to treat their needs, views, cultures and beliefs with respect.

KUW: Knowledge and Understanding of the World
Exploration and Investigation, Time, Place and Communities

▶ Finds out about past and present events in their own life, and in those of family members and other people they know. Begins to know about their own culture and beliefs, and those of other people.

▶ Finds out about and identifies the uses of everyday technology and uses information and communication technology to support their learning.

CD: Creative Development
Being Creative, Exploring Media and Materials

▶ Explores different media and responds to a variety of sensory experiences. Engages in representational play.

▶ Creates simple representations of events, people and objects, and engages in music making.

▶ Tries to capture experiences, using a variety of different media.

▶ Explores colour, texture, shape, form and space in two or three dimensions.

▶ Expresses and communicates ideas, thoughts and feelings using a range of materials, suitable tools, imaginative and role play, movement, designing and making, and a variety of songs and musical instruments.

▶ Expresses feelings and preferences in response to artwork, drama and music, and makes some comparisons and links between different pieces. Responds to their own work and that of others when exploring and communicating ideas, feelings and preferences through art, music, dance, role play and imaginative play.

PD: Physical Development
Using Equipment and Materials

▶ Demonstrates fine motor control and coordination.

▶ Uses small and large equipment, showing a range of basic skills.

▶ Handles tools, objects, construction and malleable materials safely and with basic control.

Note: On each activity page, we have concentrated on significant goals for two or three areas of learning.

The Postman

Stories about letters are a good way of getting children enthusiastic about writing letters of their own to send to family and friends. A post box makes it even more fun!

A book to get you started – The Jolly Postman; Janet and Allan Ahlberg; Heinemann

What you need

- ▶ The *Jolly Postman* story or another story about letters
- ▶ Some used letters and their envelopes
- ▶ A local map or aerial photo (optional)
- ▶ Paper, pens and envelopes
- ▶ Home-made stamps
- ▶ A post box (make one from a big box with a slit in the front)
- ▶ A cap and bag for the post person

More useful books

The Jolly Postman: Or, Other People's Letters; Janet and Allan Ahlberg; Heinemann

The Jolly Christmas Postman; Janet and Allan Ahlberg; Puffin

A Letter to Amy; Ezra Jack Keats; Puffin

A Letter to Father Christmas; Rose Impey; Orchard

The Jolly Post Office CD ROM; Allan Ahlberg; Dorling Kindersley

What you do

1. Read the story together and look at all the letters in their envelopes.

2. Talk about how the Jolly Postman knows which letter goes to which person.

3. Now look at the letters you have colloected and talk about your address (or the address of the setting or school). How does the postman know where to take your letters? Look at a local map if you have one.

4. Now make your role-play area into a post office and have plenty of letter-writing materials in the writing area. Make sure that the letters are delivered regularly and that the sender gets a reply.

And another idea...

▶ Look at the local area on Google Earth. If you live in a town or city, you may be able to look at Google Street View images and see the children's own houses.

▶ Post a letter to yourselves by addressing it to your setting. Don't forget the postcode!

▶ Make sure the children know their own address and postcode, and have practice in saying and writing these.

▶ Ask the school secretary or the person who opens the letters in your setting if you can see what the postman brings and who it is for.

Links with EYFS goals

CLLD: Language for Communication

▶ Experiments with mark making, sometimes ascribing meaning to the marks.

▶ Uses some clearly identifiable letters to communicate meaning.

CD: Exploring Media and Materials, Being Creative

▶ Explores different media and responds to a variety of sensory experiences.

▶ Engages in representational play.

Birthdays and invitations

Making invitations to send within your setting or to parents and carers is a good start to a habit of openness and invitation for all sorts of occasions.

A book to get you started – Kipper's Birthday; Mick Inkpen; Hodder

What you need

- ▶ Thin card – several different colours
- ▶ Envelopes
- ▶ Felt pens and glue sticks

More useful books

Happy Birthday Winnie!; Valerie Thomas; OUP
Spot's Birthday Party; Eric Hill; Warne
Harry and the Dinosaurs Have a Happy Birthday; Ian Whybrow; Puffin
Happy Birthday, Jamela!; Niki Daly; Frances Lincoln
Danny's Birthday; Mike Dickinson; Scholastic

What you do

1. Read the story together, and talk about what invitations look like, why you send them and what they are for.

2. Kipper wrote invitations for his birthday. What event could the children invite someone to come to? You could have a coffee morning or concert for parents. You could invite another class or group to share a story, go for a walk, join snack time or have a teddy bear's picnic.

3. When you have decided what the event will be and who you will invite, make some invitations. Kipper got in a muddle with his invitations, so you will need to agree:

   ▶ the name of the event
   ▶ the date or day
   ▶ the time
   ▶ how many people can come
   ▶ if you need an RSVP (talk about what this is)

4. If you are working with younger children, you could make a group invitation, with everyone helping to colour or decorate a big card and each child adding their name to the inside.

5. If children are making individual invitations, talk about the sorts of designs that would suit your event – try to be accepting of all sorts of ideas!

6. Make your invitations and help the children to write the information inside. You could stick a simple template in each one, like printed invitations, so the information is organised for easy reading.

And another idea...

▶ Let the children make invitations to parent interviews, sports day and other events.

▶ Invite visitors to come and talk to the children – the dentist, the nurse, a vet – and link these with projects and topics.

▶ At the end of the year, send invitations to children who will be joining the setting to ask them to visit. Use this as an opportunity for older children to 'buddy' younger children during these visits.

▶ Have a picnic or tea party. Let the children send the invitations, make the food and get everything ready.

Links with EYFS goals

CLLD: Reading
▶ Knows that print conveys meaning.

KUW: Exploration and Investigation, Time, Place and Communities
▶ Finds out about past and present events in their own life, and in those of family members and other people they know. Begins to know about their own culture and beliefs, and those of other people.

My dad is special

Opportunities to make cards for events such as Mother's or Father's Day get children used to thinking about others and what makes them special people. Make sure every child is involved in this activity by expanding the range to grandad, big brother or uncle for those children who may need an alternative.

A book to get you started – Me and My Dad!; Alison Ritchie; Little Tiger

What you need

▶ A book about a special member of the family – this example uses *Me and My Dad!* by Alison Ritchie, but you could use a book about a Mum, a friend or another family member, particularly if there are single-parent families in your group

▶ Card, pens, decorations (sequins, stickers, ribbon etc.) and scissors

▶ Envelopes

More useful books

My Dad is Brilliant, My Mum is Fantastic and My Grandma is Wonderful; Nick Butterworth; Walker

Me and My Dad, Me and My Mum and Me and My Grandma; Helen Exley; Helen Exley Giftbooks

My Mum and My Dad; Anthony Browne; Picture Corgi

All About Me and My Grandpa and All About Me and My Grandma; Egmont

What you do

1. Read the story together and talk about what makes dads special. Give each child a chance to say what is special about their dad.

2. Let each child draw a picture of themselves with their dad, doing something special.

3. Carefully cut the pictures out, helping the children if they need it.

4. Stick these pictures to a folded card to make a greetings card.

5. If the children are younger, you could let them dictate what they would like you to write inside the card. Repeated language is very good for reading, so start the same way in all the cards:

   'My dad is special because he ...'

6. Leave space for the child to write, or mark, their own name.

7. Put the card in an envelope. Let the child write on the front before they take it home.

And another idea...

▶ Photograph the fronts and the insides of the cards for a book about dads. You could ask the children to bring a photo of their dad to stick in the book next to their card.

▶ Use this method for personalised Mother's Day cards. Let the children decide what to put on the front – they could talk about the things their own mother likes best. Some mums may not want flowers!

▶ Make friendship cards to send to other children in the group or in other groups.

▶ Make a very special birthday card for your teaching assistant or other helper by writing all the things the children say they like about them, and putting pictures or photos of all the children on the front.

Links with EYFS goals

CLLD: Writing

▶ Begins to form captions and simple sentences, sometimes using punctuation.

▶ Communicates meaning through phrases and simple sentences.

KUW: Exploration and Investigation, Time, Place and Communities

▶ Finds out about past and present events in their own life, and in those of family members and other people they know. Begins to know about their own culture and beliefs, and those of other people.

Any offers?

Making posters that ask for offers of help, expertise, objects to sell or materials is a great way to get children involved in sending messages. It's a good idea to have a think before doing this activity, so you can suggest advertising for something you really want.

A book to get you started – The Great Pet Sale; Mick Inkpen; Hodder

What you need

- Large pieces of strong paper, thin card or sheeting
- Large felt pens or paints
- Smaller paper for leaflets
- Some ideas for posters:
  - ▷ help with gardening, cooking or reading
  - ▷ donations of unwanted items, such as spare wellingtons, curtains for role-play areas, saris for dressing up or display
  - ▷ recycled materials for construction or special projects, such as: yogurt pots, fabric scraps, wool, string, foil dishes, newspapers, buttons, odd socks, guttering, drainpipes, plastic crates and water bottles
  - ▷ people to show their skills, such as: spinning, woodwork, painting, sewing, cake decorating or cooking
  - ▷ resources for gardening, such as: plant cuttings and seedlings, plastic plant pots and garden furniture.
- Magazines and catalogues for pictures
- Examples of posters (optional)

More useful books

Dogger; Shirley Hughes; Red Fox
Josie and the Cake Sale; Monica Hughes; Rigby Educational
Gardening with Kids; Martyn Cox; Ryland, Peters and Small
Grow it, Eat it; Dorling Kindersley

What you do

1. Think and talk about posters, what they are for, where you see them, and how they are made and fixed to walls, fences and posts.

2. Now think about what you need and what people in your community might be able to offer. The children will probably have some good ideas, but you may have to prompt them by asking, 'Do you remember we said we needed some...?' or '...someone to help us with...' or '...someone to show us how to...?'.

3. Decide how you are going to make your posters. What will be on them? What sort of pictures will you use? What sort of writing? How will you make the writing big enough for people to see from a distance?

4. It's a good idea to start with a big poster or two, working on these as a group, putting big sheets of paper or card on the tables or floor.

5. Now decide where you are going to put the posters so everyone can see them. Pin them up and see what happens.

And another idea...

▶ 'Find' something (a key, a purse or a soft toy) on your way to work and ask the children how they could discover who owns the object.

▶ Make posters for concerts and events in your setting.

▶ Make safety posters – road safety, Bonfire Night and safety near water.

▶ Make some recycling posters to encourage parents and children to recycle paper, glass and plastic.

Links with EYFS goals

CLLD: Writing

▶ Experiments with mark making, sometimes ascribing meaning to the marks.

▶ Uses some clearly identifiable letters to communicate meaning.

▶ Attempts writing for a variety of purposes, using features of different forms.

CD: Exploring Media and Materials – Being Creative

▶ Explores different media and responds to a variety of sensory experiences.

▶ Engages in representational play.

Get well soon

Making 'get well' cards is a good way to practise card and letter making with a purpose.

A book to get you started – Dear Daisy, Get Well Soon; Maggie Smith; Dragonfly

What you need

▶ A reason for writing – this could be:
  ▷ a soft toy or doll with a bandaged arm, leg or head
  ▷ a sick child in your group
  ▷ a member of staff who is off sick.
▶ Paper, card, pens and envelopes
▶ Catalogues, wrapping paper, magazines and appropriate printed clip art
▶ Stamps
▶ Some examples of 'get well' cards (optional)
▶ Books about hospitals or being unwell (see book list on page 72)

More useful books

How Do Dinosaurs Get Well Soon?; Jane Yolen; Picture Lions
Get Well Soon; Charlotte Hudson; Red Fox
The Get Well Soon Book; Kes Gray; Millbrook Press
Going to the Hospital; Anna Civardi; Usborne Publishing
I Don't Want to Go to Hospital; Tony Ross; Picture Lions
My First Visit to Hospital; Rebecca Hunter; Evans Brothers

What you do

1. Talk about the person or character who is ill, and what has happened to them. Be sensitive to people's feelings and avoid getting too bogged down in details that might worry the children.

2. Let the children offer their experiences of being ill: how they feel, what they need to do, who looks after them, what they have to eat, the people who visit them, etc.

3. Read a story or look at a suitable non-fiction book to get information about what happens when you are ill or have to go to hospital.

4. Look at the 'get well' cards if you have some, and talk about the sorts of pictures and words used for this sort of greeting.

5. Now let the children use the resources you have collected to make their own 'get well' cards for a real person or a toy.

And another idea...

▶ Make a hospital in your role-play area, with doctor and nurse uniforms, beds for children or toys, and plenty of bandages.

▶ Look for some free e-cards for the children by putting 'e-cards for kids' in Google. These can often be downloaded and printed for children to colour in and add their own greetings.

▶ Read some more stories about hospitals and being ill.

Links with EYFS goals

PSED:

▶ Builds relationships through gesture and talk.

▶ Communicates freely about home and community.

▶ Responds to significant experiences, showing a range of feelings when appropriate.

▶ Has a developing awareness of their own needs, views and feelings, and is sensitive to the needs, views and feelings of others.

Time for a celebration

Celebrations such as Eid, Christmas and Diwali provide opportunities for making cards with a shared purpose and different interpretations of a theme.

A book to get you started – Lighting a Lamp: A Divali Story; Jonny Zucker; Frances Lincoln

What you need

▶ A celebrations calendar
▶ Information on local festivals and celebrations that are meaningful to the children – Eid, Diwali, Chinese New Year, Christmas, Chanukah/Hanukkah etc.
▶ A current festival to celebrate – we have chosen Diwali
▶ Images of Diwali lamps and candles
▶ Rectangles of card to fold into long cards
▶ Envelopes, glue sticks and pens
▶ More books about festivals (see list below)

More useful books

The Little Book of Celebrations; Dawn Roper; Featherstone Education (A&C Black)
Celebrations; Kate Tucker; A&C Black
Festival Time! by Jonny Zucker; Frances Lincoln
Kids Around the World Celebrate!: The Best Feasts and Festivals from Many Lands; Lynda Jones; Jossey Bass

What you do

1. Tell a Diwali story and talk about the festival of light celebrated during the darkest night of November. If you haven't got a celebrations book or don't know the Diwali story, look on Google, where you can read and print lots of versions.
2. Diwali is a festival of light, or lights, where people light lots of little lamps around their houses to bring good luck and chase away the dark.
3. Talk about how light makes you feel when it gets dark in the winter.
4. Show the children some pictures of Diwali lamps. They are easy to draw, so you could let them draw their own versions on brown or coloured paper to stick on their cards, or you could make a lamp template for the children to draw round.
5. Stick the lamps on to long cards, either in a row or above one another.
6. Use paint, felt pens or gold foil to add a yellow flame to each lamp.
7. Help the children to write 'Happy Diwali' inside the card and add their name.
8. Children could give their cards to each other or take them home.

And another idea...

▶ Make some Diwali lamps.

▶ Use this idea to make Eid, Chinese New Year or other celebration cards. (Find out what Chinese or Arabic writing looks like by using Google Images or Google Web.)

▶ Make recycled Christmas cards and gift tags by cutting up last year's cards or wrapping paper.

▶ Link celebrations to cooking by writing recipes for celebration food, such as chapattis, noodles and pancakes.

Links with EYFS goals

PSED:

▶ Has a developing respect for their own culture and beliefs, and those of other people.

▶ Understands that people have different needs, views, cultures and beliefs that need to be treated with respect.

▶ Understands that they can expect others to treat their needs, views, cultures and beliefs with respect.

KUW: Exploration and Investigation – Time, Place and Communities

▶ Finds out about past and present events in their own life, and in those of family members and other people they know. Begins to know about their own culture and beliefs, and those of other people.

Secret writing

Secrets and secret messages are good ways of capturing the interest of children, and boys often particularly enjoy making these invisible letters and pictures.

A book to get you started – The Secret Birthday Message; Eric Carle; HarperCollins

What you need

▶ White household candles or white crayons

▶ Strong paper or folded card

▶ Very thin, watery paint in dark colours

▶ Thick, soft paintbrushes (decorating brushes are ideal)

▶ Felt pens

More useful books

'Art Attack': Secret Stuff; Neil Buchanan; Dorling Kindersley

What you do

1. Talk about who leaves or sends secret messages (spies, detectives, wizards, fairies etc.) and why they are important.

2. If children haven't used this technique for 'invisible writing' before, you may want to demonstrate it simply by scribbling on a piece of paper or card with a candle or white crayon and then painting over it with the thin paint to reveal your marks.

3. Let the children practise by making pictures and patterns of their own, then painting over them.

4. Now talk about sending secret messages and letting the person who gets the message find out what it says. Younger children may find this difficult, as the best part of making these messages is revealing them!

5. The children can then decide who they want to send a secret message to. They can make small messages on small pieces of card or paper with tiny writing by sharpening the candle to a point or using a white crayon. Or they could make giant pictures working with a friend to make a surprise poster. Check their creation by holding it so the light catches the writing.

6. You could make a set of individual post boxes by sticking cereal boxes in a stack and adding names.

And another idea...

▶ Try writing with lemon juice (use a cotton bud as a pen). Put the message somewhere warm. As the juice gets warm, it will turn brown.

▶ Hide secret messages in the garden for the children to find.

▶ Use silver and gold crayons on white card, then paint with very dark blue paint for a night time or magical letter.

Links with EYFS goals

CLLD: Writing
▶ Experiments with mark making, sometimes ascribing meaning to the marks.
KUW: Exploration and Investigation – Time, Place and Communities
▶ Looks closely at similarities, differences, patterns and change.
CD: Exploring Media and Materials – Being Creative
▶ Explores colour, texture, shape, form and space in two or three dimensions.

Chick, chick, chick, chicken

Lift-the-flap cards, funny faces and simple pop ups are techniques that once you have taught them, will add to the repertoire of every child. Here is an idea for an Easter or spring greeting card that can easily be adapted for other occasions.

A book to get you started – Spot Goes to the Farm; Eric Hill; Warne

What you need

- ▶ Folded card for the greetings card
- ▶ Extra card for eggs
- ▶ Good scissors
- ▶ Glue sticks
- ▶ Felt pens or crayons
- ▶ Paper for the greeting
- ▶ An egg template (optional)

More useful books

Who's Making that Mess?; Philip Hawthorn; Usborne
Spot books; Eric Hill; Warne
Dear Zoo; Rod Campbell; Campbell Books

What you do

1. Help the children to cut out an egg shape from card, either by drawing one or using a template.
2. Make the egg really beautiful by colouring patterns on it.
3. Cut the card egg in two with a zigzag line. Some children may need to draw a cutting line; others may be able to do this without guides.
4. Now draw a chick in the middle of a folded card. Explain that the egg should cover the chick to make a good surprise.
5. Cut two small strips of card (about 7cm by 4cm) and fold them in half.
6. Stick the ends of the strips on the rounded ends of the back of the egg halves.
7. Put more glue on the other half of the strips and position the egg halves so they meet over the chick and can be lifted to reveal it (see illustration). Some children may need a bit of help here.
8. Let the cards dry while you write the messages. It's easier to write the message on a separate piece of paper and stick it in the card when the child is happy with their message or marks.

And another idea...

Use this method for:

▶ a gift box with a lid that lifts to reveal a gift
▶ a mask over a smiling face
▶ a bird over a nest of eggs or chicks
▶ a window that opens on a lovely view.

Links with EYFS goals

PD: Using Equipment and Materials

▶ Demonstrates fine motor control and coordination.
▶ Uses small and large equipment, showing a range of basic skills.
▶ Handles tools, objects, construction and malleable materials safely and with basic control.

CD: Exploring Media and Materials – Being Creative

▶ Explores different media and responds to a variety of sensory experiences.
▶ Engages in representational play.

I like you!

Providing some envelopes, stamps and, if possible, a simple post box or personal letter boxes (see page14) will provide more reasons for writing to friends in your setting. This idea also gives children an opportunity to celebrate what they like about their friends.

A book to get you started – Leon and Bob; Simon James; Walker Books

What you need

▶ Digital photos of all the children in your setting. The children will get through lots of these, so find out how to make sheets of small images of each child, by importing them into Word and re-sizing them so you can get 12 or 16 on a sheet. Black and white prints will reduce the costs, but an A4 photo sheet for each child will last a good time.

▶ Sheets of names of all the children and adults in your setting

▶ Card, pens, scissors, glue sticks and envelopes

More useful books

Best Friends; Marcia Leonard; Millbrook
My Friend: Jamal; Anna McQuinn
My Friends; Catherine Bruzzone; B Small

What you do

1. This activity can quickly become an independent part of your provision that children will return to again and again, so it's worth spending time on the introductory stages.

2. Look at all the resources together, and tell the children that they can use them whenever they want to send a letter to a friend or to an adult.

3. Practise the activity by each choosing someone to make a letter for. You may need to manage this so everyone gets a letter by making some yourself as you sit with the group!

4. Help the children to find a photo of their friend, cut it out and stick it at the top of the letter.

5. Now the children can draw a picture of their friend doing something they enjoy, or write something about them, for example, 'I like Anna because she _____'. If the child needs help, you could 'scribe' their words for them.

6. The child can then write their name, stick a printed version of their name or add a photo to the letter, before putting it in an envelope.

7. Now, if they ask you to, help them to find their friend's name from the places where they are displayed in your setting.

8. Stick the name on the envelope and post it in the class box or the child's own post box.

9. Now discuss with the children where the resources for this activity will be stored. Listen carefully to their suggestions and take them seriously. If they have helped to make the decision, they are much more likely to return to the resources and use them independently. Make sure the children know that they can use the resources at any time to write to anyone.

And another idea...

▶ Find some pictures of TV or film characters and add them to the activity.
▶ Add photos of the staff in your setting so children can write to them.
▶ Make 'thank you' letters for people who visit or let you visit them.

Links with EYFS goals

PSED:
▶ Builds relationships through gesture and talk.
▶ Has a developing awareness of their own needs, views and feelings, and is sensitive to the needs, views and feelings of others.

PD: Using Equipment and Materials
▶ Handles tools, objects, construction and malleable materials safely and with basic control.

Dear Giant, Dear Mouse

Very big and very small – letters to giants, fairies, goblins or monsters. Bring favourite characters to life as a stimulus for sending letters.

A book to get you started – The Fairy Princess and the Invitation; Jake Jackson; Flame Tree Publications

What you need

▶ Lots of favourite storybooks with popular characters, remembering the favourites of both boys and girls and current favourites in your group

▶ Paper in lots of colours, shapes and sizes

▶ Envelopes of different sizes and shapes – card shops sometimes have spare envelopes they will be pleased to give you, or ask colleagues and friends for spares they may have

▶ Pens, pencils and crayons – lots of different sizes from giant pencils to tiny felt pens

▶ Stickers, stamps etc.

More useful books

Dear Greenpeace; Simon James; Walker
The Fairy Princess and the Invitation; Jake Jackson; Flame Tree Publications
Lottie's Letter; Gordon Snell, Orion
Corduroy Writes a Letter (Paperback); Alison Inches; Puffin
Mouse Letters/Book and Tiny Letters; Michelle Cartlidge; Dutton

What you do

1. Look at all the stories together. You could choose one and all make letters for the same character (this makes it easier to construct a response) or you could give free choice of story to individual children.

2. Decide together where the character lives, and what sort of things the children would like to ask or tell them. Discuss what fairytale characters do, what colour paper they might like, and what the children might want to say in their letter. This sort of suggestion might help:

   ▶ A tiny letter to say you hope the fairies didn't get too wet in the storm last week.

   ▶ A great big letter to a giant to ask him not to walk on people's houses and not to shout so much.

   ▶ A letter to a wizard asking for a recipe for a spell.

   ▶ A thank you letter to the Tooth Fairy.

3. Remind the children to put their name at the end of the letter, especially if you are intending to arrange replies!

4. Let the children write their letters and put them in envelopes. You could show them how to make a matching envelope from a square of paper by folding in the four corners and sticking them down.

5. Help them to put the address on the envelope. Making up addresses is a very good creative activity!

8. You can decide whether to reply to the children's cards – they will be absolutely delighted if they find the card has disappeared the next day and a reply is left there a day or two later.

Links with EYFS goals

PD: Using Equipment and Materials
▶ Demonstrates fine motor control and coordination.
▶ Handles tools, objects, construction and malleable materials safely and with basic control.

CD: Exploring Media and Materials – Being Creative
▶ Explores different media and responds to a variety of sensory experiences.
▶ Engages in representational play.
▶ Tries to capture experiences, using a variety of different media.

Sticky fixers

Post-it notes are a good way of encouraging less-confident children to write short messages and labels. They are also good for reminders.

A book to get you started – This is the only book we can find and it seems to have lots of ideas! Post-it Ideas That Stick!: 222 Ingenious, Creative, Practical and Simply Preposterous Ways of Using Post-it Notes; The Post-it Notes Team; Fireside Books

What you need

▶ Post-it notes – all shapes, colours and sizes – look in pound shops and bargain stationers for good value packs

▶ Felt pens

▶ An old fridge door or smooth plastic tray to stick Post-its to (optional)

What you do

1. Prepare for this activity by making some example Post-it notes or collecting some from colleagues or family.
2. Talk to the children about the examples you have.
   Discuss the different uses of Post-it notes they have seen or experienced. These may include:

   ▶ reminders
   ▶ phone messages
   ▶ adverts
   ▶ lists

   ▶ prices
   ▶ phone numbers or email addresses
   ▶ addresses and

   ▶ postcodes
   ▶ observations.

3. Now let each child take some Post-it notes and decide what they are going to collect. They could:

   ▶ ask everyone for their phone number or postcode
   ▶ collect numbers from the environment or car number plates
   ▶ make lists of what they are going to do
   ▶ remind themselves (or you) of things needed for the following day
   ▶ write all the words they know.

4. Leave plenty of Post-it notes in different places in your setting:

   ▶ in the writing or mark-making area
   ▶ in the role-play area
   ▶ in the number or maths area
   ▶ in an outdoor writing box or basket.

And another idea...

▶ Use Post-it notes to record the children's achievements. Many of you already do this, but often you don't show the child or read them what you have written about them. If you begin to do this routinely, the children will get more involved in their own learning.

Links with EYFS goals

CLLD: Writing

▶ Experiments with mark making, sometimes ascribing meaning to the marks.
▶ Uses some clearly identifiable letters to communicate meaning.
▶ Writes own name and other words from memory.
▶ Holds a pencil and uses it effectively to form recognisable letters, most of which are correctly formed.
▶ Attempts writing for a variety of purposes, using features of different forms.
▶ Uses phonic knowledge to write simple regular words and make phonetically plausible attempts at more complex words.

Remember, remember

Lists and reminders are important reasons for writing, whether these are for the whole group or individuals. Making lists helps children to feel involved in planning for learning and for what is going to happen. This example shows how you can use lists to help with preparation for a visit to the park, but you can use the idea for hundreds of other reasons too.

A book to get you started – Don't Forget the Bacon; Pat Hutchins; Red Fox

What you need

▶ A flip chart or a big piece of paper clipped to an easel (don't be tempted to use an interactive whiteboard for this – it needs to be paper!)

▶ Pens

▶ A reason for listing!

More useful books

The Longest Christmas List Ever; Gregg Spiridellis; Hyperion
The Christmas List; Susan K. Leigh; Concordia

What you do

1. Read the story and talk about why making lists is a good idea. You could share your own lists of things to do or your shopping list.

2. Talk with the children about going to the park for a walk.

3. Write down all their suggestions, even those you would not have thought of.

And another idea...

▶ Make lists for each event you plan – celebrations, parties, parents' evenings and visits.

▶ As you start a new topic, make a list of the things you have in your setting that you could use for the new topic. This list might include small world figures, books, DVDs, fabrics, music etc.

▶ When you change your role-play area, perhaps to support your current topic or theme, talk with the children about what they need and make a list. What do you need for a hospital, a farm, a spaceship, or a cave?

▶ Make lists and reminders at the end of the day to remind you of things left unfinished or things the children need to experience. Encourage the children to share their intentions for the next day – what they want to do, who they want to play with etc. List the children who have not yet joined an activity/made a card/done cooking. Add reminders to yourselves about resources and activities you need to prepare or plan for.

Links with EYFS goals

CLLD: Reading

▶ Knows that print conveys meaning.
▶ Recognises a few familiar words.
▶ Knows that, in English, print is read from left to right and top to bottom.

CLLD: Writing

▶ Experiments with mark making, sometimes ascribing meaning to the marks.
▶ Uses some clearly identifiable letters to communicate meaning.
▶ Represents some sounds correctly in writing.
▶ Writes own name and other words from memory.

Be my pen-friend

Pen-friends can be just a room away, or in another street or even another country. Writing to children in other schools or settings is made easier by email and digital photography, when children can have an instant pictorial response to their letters and messages. This example shows how even in neighbouring schools, groups of children can become successful pen-friends.

A book to get you started – Pakistan (Letters from Around the World); David Cumming; Cherrytree Books

What you need

▶ A willing and reliable contact (you must make this contact before raising children's expectations)

▶ Paper, pens and envelopes

▶ A camera

▶ Access to a computer with email (optional)

More useful books

Greece (Letters from Around the World) (other titles also on Pakistan, Spain, South Africa and many other countries); David Cumming; Cherrytree Books

My Pen Pal Pat; Lisa Papademetriou; Millbrook

Older children may enjoy – Dear Whiskers; Ann Nagda; Frances Lincoln

What you do

1. You really need to prepare for this activity by contacting another practitioner and arranging to be involved together. This could be:
   ▶ another group in your school
   ▶ a neighbouring school or setting
   ▶ a school in a very different environment – in the country if you work in a city, in a very small group if you work in a very big setting
   ▶ a school or setting in a different country.

2. You also need to let parents know what you are doing, and make sure they are happy about letters and photos going between two settings.

3. Whole group activities are best to start with and will continue to bring the best experiences for the younger children.

4. Try to have some photos of the children from your partner setting to show the children. This will make the experience real for them.

5. For a starter activity, you could take photos of each child in your group, print or stick them on a big sheet of paper and let each child write their name under their own picture.

6. Send your photos to your partner school or setting. Don't miss the opportunity to talk about where they are, their address, their postcode etc. Use a local map, an atlas or even Google Earth to look for their address and what their setting looks like. The success of this activity depends on making the partner setting and children as real and recognisable as you can.

And another idea...

▶ Send some emails. These are more instant and will reinforce the relationship. You could attach photos of what you are doing and what your setting looks like at different times of the year.

Links with EYFS goals

KUW: Exploration and Investigation – Time, Place and Communities
▶ Finds out about past and present events in their own life, and in those of family members and other people they know. Begins to know about their own culture and beliefs, and those of other people.

PSED:
▶ Has a developing respect for their own culture and beliefs, and those of other people.
▶ Understands that people have different needs, views, cultures and beliefs that need to be treated with respect.
▶ Understands that they can expect others to treat their needs, views, cultures and beliefs with respect.

Wish you were here

Postcards are great to send and to receive, especially when you draw your own pictures. Great postcards can celebrate the memories of where you have been as well as being sent while you are there, so it's a good activity for just after a break or holiday period.

A book to get you started – Postcards from Dora the Explorer; Nickelodeon; Simon and Schuster

What you need

▶ Some examples of postcards, preferably those that have writing on them and have been sent

▶ Blank postcards (buy these in packs or make your own from white card)

▶ Pens

▶ Fake or real stamps

More useful books

At the Beach; Roland Harvey; Allen and Unwin
Books of postcards (often available from bargain bookstores)

What you do

1. Show your example postcards to the children and read the messages.

2. Talk together about what they know about postcards.

3. Now suggest that the children make some postcards of their own, showing their favourite places from their holidays. Talk about what they can put in the picture and what they really liked about their holiday.

4. Fine felt pens are best for drawing the pictures on postcards.

5. When these are complete, ask each child who they would like to send their postcard to. They could send them to their family, to friends or to adults in your group or setting.

6. Make a space on one of your display boards to show the postcards that have been sent within your group.

And another idea...

▶ Collect postcards from charity shops and rummage sales, so the children can explore the different scenes and places.

▶ Address some postcards with the address of your setting and give each child a postcard to take on holiday. They can draw or write their card on holiday and send it back through the post so it has arrived when they come back. This gives lots of opportunities for talking about how the cards got back!

▶ Make a role-play postcard shop and make postcards from pictures in holiday brochures.

Links with EYFS goals

CLLD: Reading
▶ Is developing an interest in books.
▶ Knows that print conveys meaning

CLLD: Writing
▶ Experiments with mark making, sometimes ascribing meaning to the marks.

Me and my home

Making a whole book by yourself is big step which sometimes needs some help. Looking at books about houses and homes may help in getting children started

A book to get you started – My Home (Board book); Rod Campbell

What you need

► A4 paper – two sheets for each book
► Pens, pencils and crayons
► A photo of each child

More useful books

My Home and My Family; Lisa Bullard; Picture Window Books
In My Home; Mari C. Schuh; Pebble Books

What you do

1. Make some simple books by folding two sheets of A4 paper together to make eight pages. You will need a book for each child.

2. Talk with the children about their houses and homes, who lives there and what their homes are like.

3. Show the children the blank books and explain that you are going to help each of them to make their own book about their home.

4. Start by taking a photo of each child (or the children could take photos of each other). Print the photos and help the children to stick their own photo on the front of their book and write their name.

5. Now talk with the children about what they will put on the other pages of their book. They could add:

   ▶ their house
   ▶ their bedroom
   ▶ their garden
   ▶ their family

   ▶ their favourite toy
   ▶ their TV with their favourite programme on the screen
   ▶ the food they eat.

6. When the books are complete, read them together and encourage the children to read them to each other.

And another idea...

▶ Make simple books like these and leave a supply in the writing corner.

▶ Show the children how to make their own books with different numbers of pages.

▶ Make a house book with pictures of different sorts of houses, flats and other places to live.

▶ Lend children a cheap digital camera to take home so they can take their own pictures of their homes and families to make into books, *PowerPoint* presentations or displays.

Links with EYFS goals

PSED:

▶ Builds relationships through gesture and talk.

▶ Communicates freely about home and community.

KUW: Exploration and Investigation – Time, Place and Communities

▶ Finds out about past and present events in their own life, and in those of family members and other people they know. Begins to know about their own culture and beliefs, and those of other people.

Zigzag through the day

Zigzag books are easy to make, and children can do this independently once you have shown them how. This example uses a simple zigzag design to take the children through their day.

A book to get you started – Going to School (Usborne First Experiences); Anna Civardi; Usborne

What you need

▶ A4 paper
▶ Pens and crayons

More useful books

Rosie's First Day at School; Rosemary Stones; Happy Cat
Starting School; Janet Ahlberg; Puffin
Lucy and Tom Go to School; Shirley Hughes; Puffin
My First Day at Nursery School; Becky Edwards; Bloomsbury

What you do

1. Make some zigzag books by folding A4 paper in half lengthways and cutting along the fold to make two strips.

2. Fold each strip in half, bringing the short edges together. Then fold each short edge back to the middle. This should make a zigzag book with four pages on each side. The books will stand up on a window-sill or they will fold into a real book when you lay them flat.

3. Check that the children start with the 'cover' page first – the page at the front of the zigzag with the book turned so this page opens like a book.

4. The children can decide whether they will put their name, a picture of their face or their photo on the front.

5. Now talk about all the things they do during the day and help them to think of what they do first in the morning – they may say, 'Wake up', 'Get up', 'Get dressed', 'Have breakfast' or something unexpected!

6. They can draw themselves doing this on the first page of their book, then continue to move through the day, drawing a picture for each of the things they do. Don't worry if they don't remember everything – the aim is to fill the book with pictures in a sequence during the day, completing the book with bedtime.

7. When the books are finished, read them together, and share them with the other children at group times and with parents at the end of the day.

And another idea...

▶ Have a zigzag book day when the children make a book each and you stop every hour to draw what you have been doing since you last filled a page. This is very good for sequencing and recall.

Links with EYFS goals

CLLD: Reading

▶ Knows that print conveys meaning.

▶ Shows an understanding of the elements of stories, such as main character, sequence of events and openings.

▶ Retells narratives in the correct sequence, drawing on language patterns of stories.

KUW: Exploration and Investigation – Time, Place and Communities

▶ Finds out about past and present events in their own life, and in those of family members and other people they know. Begins to know about their own culture and beliefs, and those of other people.

A book for a baby

Making books for younger children, either in a nursery or at home, is a real opportunity to make a contribution, either to their previous setting or to other young children.

A book to get you started – The Very Hungry Caterpillar; Eric Carle; Puffin

What you need

▶ Small card pages for the books
▶ Felt pens and scissors
▶ Stickers, wrapping paper and magazine or catalogue pictures
▶ Clear sticky-backed book covering film or access to a laminating machine
▶ Masking tape or duct tape
▶ Some simple board or bath books as examples

More useful books

Head, Shoulders, Knees and Toes...; Annie Kubler; Child's Play
That's Not My Lion; Fiona Watt; Usborne

What you do

1. Look at the baby books together and talk about why they are made the way they are.

2. Suggest that the children could make some baby books and talk about who they could give them to: local nurseries, clinics and doctors' surgeries, baby brothers and sisters etc.

3. Now choose pictures to make the pages of the book, helping the children to pick pictures that the babies might like, and stick them on the card pages.

4. The pages need to be protected with covering film or lamination (libraries and many schools have laminating facilities).

5. When the pages have been laminated, you may want to trim the corners of the pages to round them, so babies won't hurt their hands or mouths when they are using the books.

6. Use masking tape or duct tape to stick the pages together into a spine, and finish the book with some duct tape to protect the binding.

7. Take the children with you to deliver the books to a local nursery or clinic.

And another idea...

▶ Make some baby books in cheap photo albums, the small sort with plastic pockets. You can often find these in bargain or 'pound' shops.

▶ Older children may like to make baby books with simple stories and illustrate them with their own pictures.

▶ Make a book of baby photos by asking the children to bring in a photo of themselves when they were a baby. You may need to photocopy some, or ask parents to send a digital photo for you to import. As you make the book, add a photo of each child as they look now.

Links with EYFS goals

PD: Using Equipment and Materials

▶ Demonstrates fine motor control and coordination.

▶ Uses small and large equipment, showing a range of basic skills.

▶ Handles tools, objects, construction and malleable materials safely and with basic control.

PSED:

▶ Responds to significant experiences, showing a range of feelings when appropriate.

▶ Has a developing awareness of their own needs, views and feelings, and is sensitive to the needs, views and feelings of others.

Scrapbooks

A book of pictures of a favourite subject, animal or character gives children a real sense of ownership of their work. These books can be constructed over time, with contributions from home as well as your setting

A book to get you started – My Very Special Scrapbook (Paperback); Eric Carle; Puffin

What you need

▶ Home-made books with ten to twenty pages, or cheap, readymade scrapbooks – look in bargain stationer shops or 'pound' shops for cheap ones.
▶ Scissors
▶ Glue sticks
▶ Lots of picture sources:
  ▷ magazines and comics (look in car boot sales and rummage sales for National Geographic and other specialist magazines)
  ▷ wrapping paper
  ▷ clip art
  ▷ stickers and scraps (you can find sheets of scraps in craft shops)
  ▷ birthday and other greeting cards
  ▷ second-hand books (look in libraries where you can often find sale bargains of unwanted or out-of-date books)
  ▷ free-to-download pictures from the Internet.

More useful books

Let's Start a Scrapbook for Boys (Scrapattack); Lisa Regan; Top That

What you do

1. Talk about what scrapbooks are and how you can make one to collect your favourite pictures. Don't expect the children to make a collection of just one type; the idea is to collect all the things they like!

2. You also need to make it clear that children can collect pictures anywhere and make their collection over time, bringing pictures from home as well as colleting them in your setting.

3. The children can choose a scrapbook each and decorate the cover with pictures of their own or some they cut out. They also need to put their name on their own book.

4. Now offer them as wide a collection of pictures as you can. The best scrapbooks have all sorts of pictures.

5. Let the children cut and stick until they have had enough, then decide on a place where the scrapbooks will be stored and make sure children and parents know where they are and that they can add to them at any time.

6. Some children will love these books and contribute to them frequently. Others may need more encouragement and inspiration from you by the addition of new and exciting pictures.

And another idea...

▶ Make class scrapbooks to support your topics, themes and celebrations.
▶ Make sure that as the children get older, you reflect their interests by adding relevant magazines and pictures.

Links with EYFS goals

PSED:

▶ Responds to significant experiences, showing a range of feelings when appropriate.
▶ Has a developing awareness of their own needs, views and feelings, and is sensitive to the needs, views and feelings of others.

CD: Exploring Media and Materials – Being Creative

▶ Explores different media and responds to a variety of sensory experiences.
▶ Engages in representational play.
▶ Expresses feelings and preferences in response to artwork, drama and music, and makes some comparisons and links between different pieces.
▶ Responds to own work and that of others when exploring and communicating ideas, feelings and preferences through art.

My friends

A good project for the beginning or end of a year, when individual characteristics, likes and differences can be identified and celebrated.

A book to get you started – Different Just Like Me; Lori Mitchell; Charlesbridge

What you need

- ▶ Photos of all the children in your group
- ▶ Paper
- ▶ Mirrors
- ▶ Blu-tack
- ▶ Pens and crayons, including skin coloured tones for all races and cultures
- ▶ Glue sticks
- ▶ A home-made book or bought scrapbook with enough pages for one whole page per child

More useful books

All Kinds of People: a Lift-the-Flap Book; Emma Damon; Tango Books
All Kinds of Bodies: a Lift-the-Flap Book; Emma Damon; Tango Books
All About Us: Activities for 3-5 Year Olds; Irene Yates; Brilliant Publications
All About Me; Catherine Bruzzone; B Small
All About Me; Hannah Mortimer; Folens
All About Me: A Hundred Things That Happened to Me Between 0 and 3; Selina Young; Orion
My Neighborhood: Places and Faces; Lisa Bullard; Picture Window Books
Self-portrait; Louise Spilsbury; Evans

What you do

1. Take photos of every child, or let the children take photos of each other.

2. Print them out, making the prints small enough to leave room on the page for a self-portrait.

3. Look at the photos together. You can spend as long as you like discussing them, sorting them according to hair colour, eye colour, boys and girls etc. This will encourage careful looking and comparison.

4. Now arrange a self-portrait place, where several children can work together without getting in each others' way. Place the mirrors so the children can see their own faces as they sit, and put felt pens, crayons and paper where they can be seen and selected. Remember, well-displayed resources will encourage children to really look and think.

5. Give sensitive support and time as small groups of children look at their own faces in the mirrors. Encourage them to look at their own photos and talk about how they will draw a self-portrait.

6. When the portraits are complete, stick each one with the photo on its own page in the book.

And another idea...

▶ Let the children bring photos of their families and homes for individual books.

Links with EYFS goals

KUW: Exploration and Investigation – Time, Place and Communities

▶ Finds out about past and present events in their own life, and in those of family members and other people they know. Begins to know about their own culture and beliefs, and those of other people.

PSED:

▶ Has a developing awareness of their own needs, views and feelings, and is sensitive to the needs, views and feelings of others.

▶ Understands that there need to be agreed values and codes of behaviour for groups of people, including adults and children, to work together harmoniously.

▶ Has a developing respect for their own culture and beliefs, and those of other people.

▶ Understands that people have different needs, views, cultures and beliefs that need to be treated with respect.

Our topic book

Try a topic book for each of your topics or themes. Start each one at the beginning of the topic and use it at the end to celebrate what the children have learned. Our example is a topic about water.

A book to get you started – Water (Learning Through Play); Avril Harpley; Scholastic

What you need

▶ A selection of fiction and non-fiction books related to your theme – we are using books about water

▶ A big scrapbook or other home-made book with plenty of pages

▶ Some relevant wrapping paper or pictures for the cover

▶ Pictures related to the theme or topic

▶ Access to a computer with Google or another search engine

▶ Pens, crayons, scissors and glue-sticks

More useful books

The Drop in My Drink: The Story of Water on Our Planet; Meredith Hooper; Frances Lincoln
Follow the Water from Brook to Ocean; Arthur Dorros; William Morrow

What you do

1. Introduce your new topic by reading a book or story together. For our water topic, we chose:
   ▷ The Little Boat; Kathy Henderson; Walker Books
   ▷ Water; Avril Harpley; Scholastic
   ▷ The Little Book of Sand and Water; Sally Featherstone; A&C Black

2. Now talk about what the children already know about water. You could make a topic web with felt pens on a big piece of paper and use this to cover your topic book.

3. Now talk with the children about the pictures, drawings, photos and words you could put in your book. You could:
   ▷ make a list of all the water words you know
   ▷ collect weather forecasts
   ▷ draw rainy pictures
   ▷ photograph puddles
   ▷ take photos of everyone's boots
   ▷ write instructions for making simple paper or wooden boats
   ▷ draw the rain cycle (search 'water cycle' on Google)
   ▷ collect all the pictures of water you can (try Google Images).

4. Everyone in your group can contribute what they know and have learned about water, finding out things at home, on the Internet or in books.

And another idea...

▶ Draw the way that water gets into our houses and what we use it for. Label the drawings.

▶ Use the topic books at parent meetings to show parents what the children have been learning.

Links with EYFS goals

KUW: Exploration and Investigation – Time, Place and Communities
▶ Finds out about past and present events in their own life, and in those of family members and other people they know. Begins to know about their own culture and beliefs, and those of other people.

CLLD: Writing
▶ Begins to form captions and simple sentences, sometimes using punctuation.

CLLD: Reading
▶ Shows an understanding of how information can be found in non-fiction texts to answer questions about where, who, why and how.

Zigzag through a story

This is the simplest book, just a zigzag of paper or thin card, which children can manage and make themselves. They are manageable ways of helping children to sequence events and stories. This example helps with the retelling of familiar traditional stories.

A book to get you started – We think Rosie's Walk; Pat Hutchins; Red Fox would be a good starter for this activity.

What you need

▶ Plenty of simple traditional storybooks – Rosie's Walk is a good one if you want all the children to think about the same story

▶ A4 paper

▶ Pens and crayons

What you do

1. Look at the story of Rosie's Walk, or let the children read their favourite stories to each other or themselves.

2. Work on the same book, or let each child choose their favourite book. It doesn't matter if more than one child chooses the same one!

3. If the children don't know how to make them, show them how to make some zigzag books by folding A4 paper in half lengthways and cutting along the fold to make two strips. (See page 45 for more instructions).

4. Check that the children start with the 'cover' page first – the page at the front of the zigzag with the book turned so this page opens like a book.

5. Now talk with the children about making a small version of their favourite story, starting on the 'cover' with a picture and their name.

6. Let the children use the book to help them with sequencing, choosing which part of the story to put on each page, and adding words of their own.

7. When the books are finished, the children can read them to each other, to adults and to their families.

8. Add the storybooks to your book area so children can see them alongside the original stories.

And another idea...

▶ Older children could work in pairs to make storybooks, taking turns to draw and write a page.

▶ Make zigzag 1 to 10 number books with sequenced numbers and objects on each page. You will need to add pages to make the book longer!

Links with EYFS goals

CLLD: Reading

▶ Is developing an interest in books.

▶ Knows that print conveys meaning.

▶ Recognises a few familiar words.

▶ Knows that, in English, print is read from left to right and top to bottom.

▶ Shows an understanding of the elements of stories, such as main character, sequence of events and openings.

▶ Reads a range of familiar and common words and simple sentences independently.

▶ Retells narratives in the correct sequence, drawing on language patterns of stories.

Holes, staples and stitches

Fixing pages together with staples, string, wool or stitching takes children to the next level of book making. This example uses the natural world as inspiration for a nature diary.

A book to get you started – Spring Nature Activities for Children; Irmgard Kutsch; Floris Books (also available are winter, summer and autumn activities in the same series)

What you need

- ▶ Books about spring
- ▶ Sheets of card for covers – A4 or A5
- ▶ Strong paper for pages – A4 or A5
- ▶ A hole punch
- ▶ Blunt needles and wool
- ▶ A small stapler
- ▶ Pens, pastels, crayons and pencils
- ▶ A camera

More useful books

Nature Diary of an Artist; Jennie Hale; A&C Black
Nature's Playground: Activities, Crafts and Games to Encourage
Your Children to Enjoy the Great Outdoors; Fiona Danks; Frances Lincoln
I Love Dirt!: 52 Activities to Help You and Your Kids Discover the Wonders of Nature; Jennifer Ward; Shambhala
Forest Schools & Outdoor Learning in the Early Years; Sara Knight; SAGE
Green Fingers and Muddy Boots: A Year in the Garden for Children and Families; Ivor John Santer; Floris Books

What you do

1. Look at a book about the seasons or about spring.
2. Go for a walk in your garden or outdoor area to look for signs of spring.
3. When you get back, look at some of the books you have collected.
4. Now suggest that the children could make their own nature diaries to record the signs of spring they see as spring continues.
5. Show them the covers and pages of a book and then demonstrate the two methods of fixing – stapling, or sewing through holes made by using the hole punch and threading wool through to fix the pages.
6. Talk about the cover of the books and let the children discuss this before they fix the pages and cover together.
7. This session should not be too long, so be aware that some children will have had enough by the time they have done the cover and made the book.
8. In further sessions, the children can record:
   ▷ spring activities they have done in the garden or park
   ▷ plants, trees, bulbs and other flowers they see
   ▷ nests, baby birds etc.
   ▷ the weather.
9. They can also look up information and pictures on the Internet, in books and magazines or at home.

And another idea...

▶ Make a class weather chart and record the weather each day in pictures and words. Children could make mini-versions for their own books.

▶ Put out bird feeders and do some bird watching through the window, or from a secret hide-out. Record what you see.

▶ Make a class nature diary and take turns to write in it, or let the children take it in turns to draw a picture each day and write or dictate what they have seen at home or in your setting.

Links with EYFS goals

KUW: Exploration and Investigation – Time, Place and Communities

▶ Finds out about past and present events in their own life, and in those of family members and other people they know. Begins to know about their own culture and beliefs, and those of other people.

PSED:

▶ Responds to significant experiences, showing a range of feelings when appropriate.

Recycled stories

Using old and worn books to make new ones is a good way of recycling and sometimes has surprising results! Keep all your old books when they are unsuitable for your book corner, or ask a local library for books they are discarding. Make sure the children know that this is a special activity and that cutting out pictures from new books is not acceptable!

A book to get you started – Each Peach Pear Plum; Janet Ahlberg; Puffin (this book presents favourite characters and stories in a new way)

What you need

▶ Plenty of pictures from old books, presented well but not separated into their separate books
▶ Glue sticks
▶ Scissors
▶ Paper and card
▶ Staplers
▶ Pens, crayons and pencils

More useful books

Lift-the-Flap Fairy Tales: The Three Little Pigs, Red Riding Hood, Jack and the Beanstalk, Cinderella and Goldilocks; Stephen Tucker, Macmillan

What you do

1. Read Each Peach Pear Plum and talk about a story that is about lots of other stories.

2. Now look at the resources you have collected. Let the children have a good look at the pictures, they will need plenty of time to go through the pictures and talk about them.

3. Make some simple books by stapling sheets of paper together, with or without card covers.

4. Encourage the children to choose one picture to start their story. Some children will select all their pictures before they start, and will know what their story is. Others will need more help and may just tell the story page by page as they work.

5. Stick the first picture on the first page. Depending on the age and maturity of the children, they may be able to write the story, you could write for them, or they could just use the pictures and tell the story out loud.

6. Continue to stick pictures in the books and tell the story. This may take more than one session.

7. When the stories are finished, don't forget to make time for the children to tell them to other people, then they could take them home or add them to your story corner or library.

8. A photo of the child on the front or back cover of the book will raise self-esteem.

And another idea...

▶ Make storybooks with pictures from comics and magazines. Superheroes are very popular, and boys will welcome the opportunity to write about their own heroes.

▶ Get some stickers (animals, people, film or TV characters etc.) and use these to make storybooks. If you choose little stickers, you can make tiny books.

Links with EYFS goals

CLLD: Reading

▶ Is developing an interest in books.

▶ Knows that print conveys meaning.

▶ Shows an understanding of the elements of stories, such as main character, sequence of events and openings.

▶ Retells narratives in the correct sequence, drawing on language patterns of stories.

Simple lift-the-flap books

Lift-the-flap books are more complex to make but children love them, and making them is a great way to develop fine motor skills. Making a book together is a good way to start.

A book to get you started – Dear Zoo; Rod Campbell; Campbell Books

What you need

- ▶ Thick card, cut in pieces about 15cm square for the pages
- ▶ Thinner card for the flaps
- ▶ Scissors
- ▶ Pens and pencils
- ▶ Masking tape
- ▶ Duct tape
- ▶ Some more Lift the Flap books

More useful books

Who's Making That Mess?, Who's Making That Smell? and Who's Making That Noise? (Lift-the-flap); Philip Hawthorn; Usborne
See Inside Your Body and **See Inside Castles** (Usborne Flap books); Katie Daynes; Usborne

What you do

1. Look at Dear Zoo and some more Lift-the-flap books.
2. Look carefully at how these books are made and talk about how the children could make some.
3. Explain that the easiest way to make a Lift-the-flap book is to make all the pages first, and that you can work on a book together.
4. Each child should choose a favourite animal and draw it in the middle of their page.
5. Next, they need to cut a big enough piece of card to cover their animal. They may need help here, and some will have more than one attempt before they get the right size and shape, but it is good experience!
6. Now they can draw on the covering piece to make it into a cage, bush, kennel or box for their animal to hide behind.
7. Finally, they can fix their flap on to the page with masking tape along one side, so they can lift it up. Masking tape is best because it can be torn easily and repositioned if it gets in the wrong place.
8. When all the children have finished their pages and practised lifting the flaps, use duct tape to fix the pages together into a book, by putting pages edge to edge, almost touching (a space between the edges will make it easier to open the book) and running a piece of tape down the join. Complete the spine by taping all the pages together.

And another idea...

▶ Write the story on the blank facing pages opposite each picture, using the format of Dear Zoo or another animal Lift-the-flap book.

▶ When the children know how to do this, leave the materials available for self-chosen book making.

▶ Provide small pictures, stickers, clip art and photos of the children for making more Lift-the-flap books.

Links with EYFS goals

PD: Using Equipment and Materials

▶ Demonstrates fine motor control and coordination.
▶ Uses small and large equipment, showing a range of basic skills.
▶ Handles tools, objects, construction and malleable materials safely and with basic control.

CD: Exploring Media and Materials – Being Creative

▶ Explores different media and responds to a variety of sensory experiences.
▶ Engages in representational play.

The day we went to...

Get in the habit of using a camera to capture images of outings and visits ready for book making. Photos will trigger memories, help with vocabulary and sequencing, and enable the children to revisit these key experiences.

A book to get you started – We Went to Visit a Farm One Day; Jane Chapman; Walker Books

What you need

- ▶ A camera
- ▶ An empty home-made book or a photo album
- ▶ A glue stick
- ▶ Pens

More useful books

Going Out; Anthony Lewis; Child's Play
We Went to Visit a Farm One Day; Jane Chapman; Walker
What if we had a farm?; Sally Featherstone/A&C Black

What you do

1. Before you go on your trip, look at a photo book together, such as What if we had a farm? (A&C Black). Talk about the photos and how photos can remind you of a visit, a holiday or a special occasion.

2. Take plenty of photos on each trip or visit. Even simple outings like walks to the park or the shops will provide real resources for language and thinking.

3. Let the children take some of the photos. They will certainly have a different view of what is important to record!

4. When you get back, download and print the photos as soon as you can.

5. Sit with the children in a place where you can spread the photos out. Give them plenty of time to look at all the photos and discuss them.

6. Talk about what happened when, and try to make the photos into a timeline or sequence of the visit.

7. Now put the photos in a book or album.

8. The children could write captions or dictate them to an adult.

And another idea...

▶ Print multiple, smaller copies of some of the photos for individual books.

▶ Put the photos on *PowerPoint* so the children can watch a slide-show on the computer or whiteboard. Be sure to add some captions so they are associating the pictures and words.

▶ Show the photo book or presentation to parents – have it running on the whiteboard at home time, or put up a sign saying 'Come and look at a photo book of our visit'.

Links with EYFS goals

KUW: Exploration and Investigation – Time, Place and Communities

▶ Finds out about past and present events in their own life, and in those of family members and other people they know. Begins to know about their own culture and beliefs, and those of other people.

PSED:

▶ Responds to significant experiences, showing a range of feelings when appropriate.

Once upon a time

Using a familiar story as a basis for book making helps with sequencing and recall. Frequent opportunities to make and read familiar stories to each other should be a part of every day. We have chosen The Gruffalo, but any story with a good narrative and a range of characters will do. Repetitive language will help children to remember the words.

A book to get you started – The Gruffalo; Julia Donaldson

What you need

- ▶ A favourite storybook
- ▶ A big blank home-made book or scrapbook
- ▶ Paper
- ▶ Felt pens and crayons
- ▶ Glue sticks

More useful books

Each Peach Pear Plum; Janet Ahlberg; Puffin

There Was an Old Lady Who Swallowed a Fly; Pam Adams; Child's Play

The Wheels on the Bus Go Round and Round; Annie Kubler; Child's Play

And for rhyming books:

Room on the Broom, The Gruffalo, A Squash and a Squeeze, Snail and the Whale, and Sharing a Shell; Julia Donaldson

Don't Put Your Finger in the Jelly Nelly, Ketchup on Your Cornflakes? and I Went to the Zoopermarket; Nick Sharratt; Scholastic

Pass the Jam, Jim; Kaye Umansky; Red Fox

What you do

1. Read the story again so the children have a reminder of what happens.
2. Now suggest that you could make your own version of the story in the big book, making a part of the story each.
3. Look at the story again so the children can decide which part they would like to contribute to. You could make a list on a flip chart or a big piece of paper of all the animals that the mouse met on his walk through the woods, the part where he meets the Gruffalo and the second time he meets the animals on the way back.
4. The children could write their names beside the one they choose.
5. Other children might like to make the picture for the cover, the back cover, the Gruffalo, the mouse or the woods. There should be plenty of choice.
6. Now the children can make their pictures to stick on the right pages in the book and write the words unaided or with your help.

N.B. Encourage 'have a go' writing, not copying from the book.

And another idea...

▶ Younger children may derail your attempts at sequencing and just stick to the part they like best – be patient and use whatever they produce to make a book with their own words as captions.

▶ Role-play resources and a few dressing-up clothes will help you to re-enact and capture the story as you tell it. You could make a photo version of any book, starring your children telling the story in your setting or garden. The dressing-up clothes don't need to be complex or expensive – children will make do with surprisingly simple objects, a few pieces of fabric and some hats.

▶ When your favourite storybooks get worn out, use the pictures to make a new version with words by the children. Put the pictures in a different order, have a different hero or villain, and tell the story in the children's own words.

Links with EYFS goals

CLLD: Reading

▶ Is developing an interest in books.

▶ Knows that print conveys meaning.

▶ Shows an understanding of the elements of stories, such as main character, sequence of events and openings.

▶ Reads a range of familiar and common words and simple sentences independently.

▶ Retells narratives in the correct sequence, drawing on language patterns of stories.

Guess what happened last Wednesday?

Making diaries, day books and timelines is a good way to record the passing of time and the events of days, weeks, seasons and years. Children will return to these time after time to remind themselves of the events they have experienced.

A book to get you started – Diary of a Wombat; Jackie French; HarperCollins

What you need

► Diaries and day books to use as examples – preferably with writing in them!

► A blank, hard-backed notebook with plain pages, the bigger the better (you can often find these in bargain stationers or 'pound' shops)

► Pens, pencils and crayons

► A calendar

More useful books

Diary of a Worm/Spider/Fly; Doreen Cronin; Harper Collins

All in a Day (Hardcover); Cynthia Rylant; Harry N Abrahams

What's the Time Mr Wolf?; Gemma Raynor; Meadowside

What's the Time, Mr. Wolf?; Annie Kubler; Child's Play

Night Monkey, Day Monkey; Julia Donaldson; Egmont

Victoria's Day; Maria de Fatima Campos; Frances Lincoln (about a day in the life of a Down's syndrome child)

What you do

1. This activity needs stamina on your part, or the children will forget about it and the purpose of the diary will be lost! Children need to feel excited about the book, so make it an enjoyable activity, not a chore. Make it voluntary and don't expect everyone to write in the diary every day.

2. Read the story together and talk about what the wombat did each day.

3. Now show the children the diaries you have collected as samples, and talk about what a diary is and who might use one.

4. Show them the empty notebook and suggest they might like to make a diary about what happens in your setting. You may want to start this activity on the day after a significant event, such as:
   ▷ a visit
   ▷ some exceptional weather
   ▷ a child or adult's birthday
   ▷ a festival or celebration.

5. Suggest that the first page should be about what happened the day before (or something exciting you are going to do the next day).

6. Now put the day and the date on the first page and let the children write and draw pictures of what happened.

7. Continue to remind the children about the diary. Leave it in the writing area and let the children know that they can write in it at any time. Don't forget to read and share what the children write and draw.

And another idea...

▶ Make a birthday diary and have a special page for each child's birthday. Make a decorative border round the page and put the child's name and a photo at the top. The other children can write or draw what they like about the 'birthday child'.

▶ Make a weather diary using symbols, photos and weather forecast information. Have a weather station in your garden and collect information about the wind and rain etc.

Links with EYFS goals

KUW: Exploration and Investigation – Time, Place and Communities

▶ Finds out about past and present events in their own life, and in those of family members and other people they know.

CD: Exploring Media and Materials – Being Creative

▶ Explores different media and responds to a variety of sensory experiences.

▶ Engages in representational play.

▶ Creates simple representations of events, people and objects.

▶ Tries to capture experiences using a variety of different media.

Virtual stories

Using computers to make books, particularly e-books, meant to be read on screen, is a good opportunity to use ICT for a real purpose. Writing emails is another way to get children involved in the art of letter writing.

A book to get you started – Winnie's New Computer; Valerie Thomas and Korky Paul; OUP

What you need

▶ A computer with a program for making books or presentations (for example *PowerPoint* or *Publisher*)

▶ Email facility and a safe list of email addresses

▶ A printer (optional)

▶ A digital camera

More useful books

2Simple produce simple software programs for young children for making postcards, books, leaflets and stories:
http://www.2simpleshop.com/2publishplus
Talking Tins, photo albums and Talking Postcards can be found at:
http://www.talkingproducts.co.uk/talking_tins_education.htm
See an almost indestructible children's still and video camera from:
www.tts-group.co.uk/tuff-cam or www.digitalblue.org.uk
My First Book about the Internet (with disk); Sharon Cromwell; Troll Communications
Arthur's Computer Disaster; Marc Brown; Little, Brown
Computer Fun for Everyone: Great Things to Do and Make with Any Computer; Elin Kordahl Saltveit; Jossey Bass

What you do

1. It's essential to make arrangements with recipients before involving children in writing and sending emails. Many children already have email addresses, and you may be able to set up email addresses for the children in your setting, so they can email each other safely. Make sure you have a very good spam filter, or get all the emails to come through you, so you can screen them.

2. *PowerPoint, Keynote* (a Macintosh version) and other simple publishing programs are available for PC Windows and Macintosh machines. Teach the children how to use these – by importing photos, adding text and drawing pictures on screen or scanning them in. Very young children can learn these techniques, often more easily than we can!

3. Read the story together and find out what happened when Winnie the Witch had a new computer.

4. Now use your ICT resources to make simple books to look at on screen or print out.

And another idea...

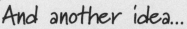

▶ Burn the children's stories on to CD so they can share them with their families and friends.

▶ Try some talking books from your library.

▶ Buy some books with CDs or DVDs and use these as models for your own stories. Watch these together on a whiteboard or computer as an alternative to, but not a replacement for, real books.

Links with EYFS goals

KUW: Exploration and Investigation – Time, Place and Communities

▶ Finds out about past and present events in their own life, and in those of family members and other people they know. Begins to know about their own culture and beliefs, and those of other people.

▶ Finds out about, and identifies the uses of, everyday technology, and uses information and communication technology to support their learning.

CLLD: Writing

▶ Attempts writing for a variety of purposes, using features of different forms.

▶ Uses phonic knowledge to write simple regular words and make phonetically plausible attempts at more complex words.

My own sketchbook

Making their own sketchbook and filling it with drawings is an exciting project for children of all ages. Make sure they understand it is theirs and they can draw whatever they like, whenever they choose. Some children will fill a book very quickly!

A book to get you started – Teaching Art to Young Children 4-9 (Paperback); Rob Barnes; Routledge

What you need

- ▶ Cartridge or good quality drawing paper
- ▶ Soft pencils and pencil crayons
- ▶ Staplers (a long-armed stapler will make this job much easier as you can staple the middle of the pages and then fold them into a booklet)
- ▶ A hole punch
- ▶ Ribbon or coloured string
- ▶ Lots of objects to decorate the front cover – pictures, scraps, stickers, sequins and braid, wrapping paper etc.
- ▶ Chairs, cushions and rugs outside

More useful books

Drawing with Children (Paperback); Mona Brookes; GP Putnams
http://www.kinderart.com/crafts/sketchbook.shtml for instructions on making a different sort of sketchbook
http://www.gis.net/scatt/sketchbook/links2.html looks at hundreds of artists' sketchbooks online

What you do

1. Talk about sketchbooks. You could look at some images from the Internet by putting 'sketchbook' or 'kids' sketchbooks online' in Google Images and choosing some images to show the children.

2. Make a sketchbook each by selecting the number of pages and then stapling or fixing them together.

3. The children should decorate the cover and add their name.

4. Now go outside and encourage them to do their first drawing of anything they see. You may have to look hard and talk about things first, but favourite places, objects, plants and games are all good things to have a go at first. Remember that some children will prefer to draw standing up; others may like to sit or even lie down to be comfortable.

5. When the children have completed their drawings, look at them together and discuss where the sketchbooks will be stored. Remind the children so they keep thinking about drawing.

And another idea...

▶ Continue your outdoor drawing sessions, and make sure the children have plenty of opportunities to choose this activity.

▶ Take the sketchbooks when you go on walks and visits.

▶ Visit your local art gallery and look at drawings or look in books.

▶ Contact your local school of art and ask if the students could come to show their sketchbooks.

▶ Set up drawing opportunities by bringing objects into the setting for children to draw. You could offer:

   ▷ a bicycle

   ▷ a vase of seasonal flowers or a pot plant

   ▷ a collection of natural objects, such as seed heads, leaves or cones.

Links with EYFS goals

CD: Exploring Media and Materials – Being Creative

▶ Explores different media and responds to a variety of sensory experiences.

▶ Engages in representational play.

▶ Creates simple representations of events, people and objects, and engages in music making.

▶ Tries to capture experiences using a variety of different media.

▶ Explores colour, texture, shape, form and space in two or three dimensions.

▶ Expresses and communicates ideas, thoughts and feelings using a range of materials, suitable tools, imaginative role-play, movement, designing and making, and a variety of songs and musical instruments.

Book list

The postman (p14)

The Jolly Postman: or, Other People's Letters; Janet and Allan Ahlberg; Heinemann

The Jolly Christmas Postman; Janet Ahlberg; Puffin

A Letter to Amy; Ezra Jack Keats; Puffin

A Letter to Father Christmas; Rose Impey; Orchard

The Jolly Post Office; Allan Ahlberg; DK

Birthdays and invitations (p16)

Happy Birthday Winnie!; Valerie Thomas; OUP

Kipper's Birthday; Mick Inkpen; Hodder

Spot's Birthday Party; Eric Hill; Warne

Harry and the Dinosaurs Have a Happy Birthday; Ian Whybrow; Puffin

Happy Birthday, Jamela!; Niki Daly; Frances Lincoln

Danny's Birthday; Mike Dickinson; Scholastic

My dad is special (p18)

Me and My Dad!; Alison Ritchie; Little Tiger

My Dad is Brilliant, My Mum is Fantastic and My Grandma is Wonderful; Nick Butterworth; Walker

Me and My Dad, Me and My Mum and Me and My Grandma; Helen Exley; Helen Exley Giftbooks

My Mum and My Dad; Anthony Browne; Picture Corgi

All About Me and My Grandpa and All About Me and My Grandma; Egmont

Any offers (p20)

Dogger; Shirley Hughes; Red Fox

The Great Pet Sale; Mick Inkpen; Hodder

Josie and the Cake Sale; Monica Hughes; Rigby Educational

Gardening with Kids; Martyn Cox; Ryland, Peters and Small

Grow it, Eat it; Dorling Kindersley

Get well soon (p22)

How Do Dinosaurs Get Well Soon?; Jane Yolen; Picture Lions

Get Well Soon; Charlotte Hudson; Red Fox

The Get Well Soon Book; Kes Gray; Millbrook Press

Dear Daisy, Get Well Soon; Maggie Smith; Dragonfly

Going to the Hospital; Anna Civardi; Usborne Publishing

I Don't Want to Go to Hospital; Tony Ross; Picture Lions

My First Visit to Hospital; Rebecca Hunter; Evans Brothers

Time for a celebration (p24)

The Little Book of Celebrations; Dawn Roper; Featherstone Education (A&C Black)

Celebrations; Kate Tucker; A&C Black

Lighting a Lamp: A Divali Story (and other celebration titles); Jonny Zucker; Frances Lincoln

Kids Around the World Celebrate!: The Best Feasts and Festivals from Many Lands; Lynda Jones; Jossey Bass

Secret writing (p26)

The Secret Birthday Message; Eric Carle; HarperCollins

'Art Attack': Secret Stuff; Neil Buchanan; Dorling Kindersley

Chick, chick, chick, Chicken! (p28)

Who's Making That Mess?; Philip Hawthorn; Usborne

Spot Goes to the Farm; Eric Hill; Warne

Dear Zoo; Rod Campbell; Campbell Books

I like you (p30)

Best Friends; Marcia Leonard; Millbrook

My Friend: Jamal; Anna McQuinn

Leon and Bob; Simon James; Walker

My Friends; Catherine Bruzzone; B Small

Dear Giant, Dear Mouse (p32)

Dear Greenpeace; Simon James; Walker

The Fairy Princess and the Invitation; Jake Jackson; Flame Tree Publications

Lottie's Letter (Illustrated) (Paperback); Gordon Snell; Orion

Corduroy Writes a Letter (Paperback); Alison Inches; Puffin

Mouse Letters/Book and Tiny Letters; Michelle Cartlidge; Dutton

Sticky fixers (p34)

Post-it Ideas That Stick!: 222 Ingenious, Creative, Practical and Simply Preposterous Ways of Using Post-it Notes; The Post-it Notes Team; Fireside Books

Remember, remember (p36)

The Longest Christmas List Ever (Hardcover); Gregg Spiridellis; Hyperion

The Christmas List (Hardcover); Susan K. Leigh; Concordia

Be my pen-friend (p38)

Greece (Letters from Around the World) (also in the series: Pakistan, Spain, South Africa and many other countries (Hardcover); David Cumming; Cherrytree Books

My Pen Pal Pat; Lisa Papademetriou; Millbrook

Older children may enjoy – Dear Whiskers; Ann Nagda; Frances Lincoln

Wish you were here (p40)
Postcards from Dora; Nickelodeon; Simon and Schuster
At the Beach; Roland Harvey; Allen and Unwin
Books of postcards

Me and my home (p42)
My Home (Board book); R. Campbell
My Home and My Family; Lisa Bullard; Picture Window Books
In My Home; Mari C. Schuh; Pebble Books
My Family Tree Book; Catherine Bruzzone; B Small

Zigzag through the day (p44)
Going to School (Usborne First Experiences); Anna Civardi; Usborne
Rosie's First Day at School; Rosemary Stones; Happy Cat
Starting School; Janet Ahlberg; Puffin
Lucy and Tom Go to School; Shirley Hughes; Puffin
My First Day at Nursery School; Becky Edwards; Bloomsbury

A book for a baby (p46)
The Very Hungry Caterpillar; Eric Carle; Puffin
Head, Shoulders, Knees and Toes...; Annie Kubler; Child's Play
That's Not My Lion; Fiona Watt; Usborne

Scrapbooks (p48)
My Very Special Scrapbook (Paperback); Eric Carle; Puffin
Let's Start a Scrapbook for Boys (Scrapattack) (Paperback); Lisa Regan; Top That

My friends (p50)
Different Just Like Me; Lori Mitchell; Charlesbridge
All Kinds of People: a Lift-the-Flap Book; Emma Damon; Tango Books
All Kinds of Bodies: a Lift-the-Flap Book; Emma Damon; Tango Books
All About Us: Activities for 3-5 Year Olds; Irene Yates; Brilliant Publications
All About Me; Catherine Bruzzone; B Small
All About Me; Hannah Mortimer; Folens
All About Me: A Hundred Things That Happened to Me Between 0 and 3; Selina Young; Orion
My Neighborhood: Places and Faces; Lisa Bullard; Picture Window Books
Self-portrait; Louise Spilsbury; Evans

Our topic book (p52)
The Drop in My Drink: The Story of Water on Our Planet; Meredith Hooper; Frances Lincoln
Follow the Water from Brook to Ocean; Arthur Dorros; William Morrow

Water (Learning Through Play) (Paperback); Avril Harpley; Scholastic

Zigzag through a story (p54)
Rosie's Walk; Pat Hutchins; Red Fox

Holes, staples and stitches (p56)
Nature Diary of an Artist (Hardcover); Jennie Hale; A&C Black

Nature's Playground: Activities, Crafts and Games to Encourage Your Children to Enjoy the Great Outdoors; Fiona Danks; Frances Lincoln

I Love Dirt!: 52 Activities to Help You and Your Kids Discover the Wonders of Nature (Paperback); Jennifer Ward; Shambhala

Forest Schools & Outdoor Learning in the Early Years (Paperback); Sara Knight; SAGE

Green Fingers and Muddy Boots: A Year in the Garden for Children and Families; Ivor John Santer; Floris Books

Recycled stories (p58)
Lift-the-Flap Fairy Tales: The Three Little Pigs, Red Riding Hood, Jack and the Beanstalk, Cinderella and Goldilocks; Stephen Tucker; MacMillan

Simple lift-the-flap book (p60)
Who's Making that Mess?, Who's Making That Smell? and Who's Making That Noise? (Lift-the-flap); Philip Hawthorn; Usborne

See Inside Your Body and See Inside Castles (Usborne Flap books); Katie Daynes; Usborne

Dear Zoo; Rod Campbell; Campbell Books

The day we went to... (p62)
Going Out; Anthony Lewis; Child's Play

We Went to Visit a Farm One Day; Jane Chapman; Walker

What if We Went to the Farm?; Featherstone/A&C Black

Once upon a time (p64)
Each Peach Pear Plum; Janet Ahlberg; Puffin

There Was an Old Lady Who Swallowed a Fly; Pam Adams; Child's Play

The Wheels on the Bus Go Round and Round; Annie Kubler; Child's Play

Room on the Broom, The Gruffalo, A Squash and a Squeeze, Snail and the Whale and Sharing a Shell; Julia Donaldson

Don't Put Your Finger in the Jelly Nelly, Ketchup on Your Cornflakes? and I Went to the Zoopermarket; Nick Sharratt; Scholastic

Pass the Jam, Jim; Kaye Umansky

Guess what happened last Wednesday (p66)

Diary of a Wombat; Jackie French; HarperCollins

Diary of a Worm; Doreen Cronin; HarperCollins

Diary of a Spider; Doreen Cronin; HarperCollins

Diary of a Fly; Doreen Cronin; HarperCollins

All in a Day (Hardcover); Cynthia Rylant; Harry N Abrahams

What's the Time Mr Wolf?; Gemma Raynor; Meadowside

What's the Time, Mr. Wolf?; Annie Kubler, Child's Play

Night Monkey, Day Monkey; Julia Donaldson; Egmont

Victoria's Day; Maria de Fatima Campos; Frances Lincoln (about a day in the life of a Down's syndrome child)

Rosie's Walk; Pat Hutchins; Puffin

Virtual stories (p68)

Winnie's New Computer; Valerie Thomas and Korky Paul; OUP

My First Book about the Internet (with disk); Sharon Cromwell; Troll Communications

Arthur's Computer Disaster; Marc Brown; Little Brown

Computer Fun for Everyone: Great Things to Do and Make with Any Computer (Paperback); Elin Kordahl Saltveit; Jossey Bass

My own sketchbook (p70)

Drawing with Children (Paperback); Mona Brookes; GP Putnams

Teaching Art to Young Children 4-9 (Paperback); Rob Barnes; Routledge

http://www.kinderart.com/crafts/sketchbook.shtml

http://www.gis.net/scatt/sketchbook/links2.html (Hundreds of artists' sketchbooks online)

Equipment

Long-armed stapler
From stationers or educational supply catalogues

Needles
Children's needles with big eyes, in plastic and metal are available from Education Suppliers and on the Internet – just put 'children's sewing needles' in a search engine.

Needle threaders
These simple devices really help children and adults with threading needles; get them from craft shops and sewing suppliers.

Scissors
Invest in good scissors. Fiskars make good quality scissors for adults and round-ended ones suitable for children. Left-handed scissors are a useful addition.

There are lots of training scissor designs, you may have to experiment to find ones that suit you and the children, but they are very useful for younger or less dextrous children.

Patterned scissors

Brusho (www.colourcraftltd .com)
Brusho is a concentrated water based colouring powder that is safe to use with children. It has a really great range of colours, particularly for cold-dying fabrics or paper, and for 'secret writing', but it does stain, so be careful when using it, and supervise carefully.

Food colouring
You can get food colouring in big bottles from TTS at **www.tts-group.co.uk**. Food colouring is good for secret writing as it is safe if licked from fingers.

Single hole punches
These are useful for punching holes in thick card or leather – you can get ones with a single hole and others with multiple sizes.

If you have found this book useful you might also like ...

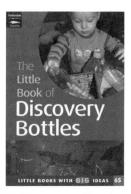

LB Discovery Bottles
ISBN 978-1-9060-2971-5

LB Christmas
ISBN 978-1-9022-3364-2

LB Making Poetry
ISBN 978-1-4081-1250-2

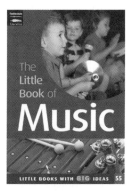

LB Music
ISBN 978-1-9041-8754-7

The Little Books Club

There is always something in Little Books to help and inspire you.
Packed full of lovely ideas, Little Books meet the need for exciting and
practical activities that are fun to do, address the Early Learning Goals
and can be followed in most settings. Everyone is a winner!

We publish 5 new Little Books a year. Little Books Club members receive
each of these 5 books as soon as they are published for a reduced price.
The subscription cost is £37.50 – a one off payment that buys
the 5 new books for £7.50 instead of £8.99 each.

In addition to this, Little Books Club Members receive:
· Free postage and packing on anything ordered from the
  Featherstone catalogue
· A 15% discount voucher upon joining which can be used to buy any
  number of books from the Featherstone catalogue
· Members price of £7.50 on any additional Little Book purchased
· A regular, free newsletter dealing with club news, special offers and
  aspects of Early Years curriculum and practice
· All new Little Books on approval - return in good condition within 30
  days and we'll refund the cost to your club account

Call 020 7440 2446 or email: littlebooks@acblack.com for
an enrolment pack. Or download an application form from our website:

www.acblack.com/featherstone

The **Little Books** series consists of:

All Through the Year
Bags, Boxes & Trays
Bricks and Boxes
Celebrations
Christmas
Circle Time
Clay and Malleable Materials
Clothes and Fabrics
Colour, Shape and Number
Cooking from Stories
Cooking Together
Counting
Dance
Dance, with music CD
Discovery Bottles
Dough
50
Fine Motor Skills
Fun on a Shoestring
Games with Sounds
Growing Things
ICT
Investigations
Junk Music
Language Fun
Light and Shadow

Listening
Living Things
Look and Listen
Making Books and Cards
Making Poetry
Mark Making
Maths Activities
Maths from Stories
Maths Songs and Games
Messy Play
Music
Nursery Rhymes
Outdoor Play
Outside in All Weathers
Parachute Play
Persona Dolls
Phonics
Playground Games
Prop Boxes for Role Play
Props for Writing
Puppet Making
Puppets in Stories
Resistant Materials
Role Play
Sand and Water
Science through Art
Scissor Skills

Sewing and Weaving
Small World Play
Sound Ideas
Storyboards
Storytelling
Seasons
Time and Money
Time and Place
Treasure Baskets
Treasureboxes
Tuff Spot Activities
Washing Lines
Writing

All available from
www.acblack.com/featherstone